The Sounds of Music

By L. C. Casterline
Illustrations by Lane Yerkes

Gareth Stevens Publishing
A WORLD ALMANAC EDUCATION GROUP COMPANY

Please visit our web site at: www.garethstevens.com
For a free color catalog describing Gareth Stevens Publishing's
list of high-quality books and multimedia programs,
call 1-800-542-2595 (USA) or 1-800-387-3178 (Canada).
Gareth Stevens Publishing's fax: (414) 332-3567.

Library of Congress Cataloging-in-Publication Data available upon request from publisher.
Fax (414) 336-0157 for the attention of the Publishing Records Department.

ISBN 0-8368-4100-X

First published in 2004 by
Gareth Stevens Publishing
A World Almanac Education Group Company
330 West Olive Street, Suite 100
Milwaukee, Wisconsin 53212 USA

Copyright © 2004 by Nancy Hall, Inc.

Gareth Stevens editor: Barbara Kiely Miller
Gareth Stevens art direction: Tammy Gruenewald

Printed in the United States of America

1 2 3 4 5 6 7 8 9 08 07 06 05 04

Making Music

Music comes from all over
the world. There are almost
as many different kinds of
music as there are performers.
Some performers play
musical instruments.
Others sing or dance.
How do you make music?

When the rock band runs onstage, everyone cheers. The lead guitar sounds the first note. Then the bass guitar, keyboard, and drums join in. Doesn't the heavy beat make you want to clap your hands and dance?

Jazz music can be cool and slow — or hot and fast!
Some jazz musicians make up brand-new music
while they're onstage, playing the bass fiddle,
clarinet, and trumpet.

Scritchy-scratch

Clackety clack!

Did you know that you can make music with a washboard and a pair of spoons? The scritchy-scratch of the washboard and clackety-clack of the spoons keep time while the country singers carry the tune.

The accordion is also called a squeeze box, because you squeeze the two sides together to make music. Come on, let's dance to the polka!

In Spain, the guitar is used to play sweet, sad music that can make you cry — or proud flamenco songs that will have you snapping your fingers like castanets.

Flamenco dancers stand up straight, stamping
their feet and clicking their castanets in time
to the music.

9

The next time you go to a parade, look for the tuba players marching in the back of the band. Their big, brass horns make deep, round sounds.

The harpist plays delicate music by plucking the strings of the harp. Harp music can be as soothing as gentle rain tapping on the window.

The orchestra is tuning up for a concert. The
conductor stands in front, a baton in one hand. He
raises his arms, and everything goes quiet. Then he
brings them down, and the orchestra begins to play.

All the different instruments — singing violins,
trilling flutes, tootling brassy horns, and booming
kettledrums — come together, weaving the different
parts of the music into one big symphony of sound.

Music can make you feel like singing and dancing, laughing, or crying. A roll of drums can make you think of horses galloping across the plains. The trill of the flute may remind you of birds singing in the dawn. Music is everywhere for you to enjoy. All you have to do is open your heart and listen.

About the Author

The author of several children's books, L. C. Casterline has also been a children's book editor for many years. She and her cat, Josephine, live just outside New York City.

About the Illustrator

Lane Yerkes graduated from the Philadelphia College of Art and served four years in the U.S. Navy. He has illustrated children's books, textbooks, and magazine and newspaper articles, as well as created fabric designs, posters, and logos. Yerkes lives on the southwest coast of Florida, not far from the Everglades.